How to Write a Personal Statement:

The 5 Step Formula

Jonty Purvis

About the Author

My name is Jonty Purvis. I graduated from Cambridge University in 2017 and I have just completed an MBA. After graduating, I started my own private tuition business (Revision Hive) based in London. I specialize in teaching essay writing techniques to GCSE, A Level, and University students in a number of subjects such as French, History, English, and Geography. We have recently expanded, and now offer tuition in every major subject, including Science and Maths. This service also provides personal statement help and mock interviews for Oxbridge students and medical students. Our simple but effective techniques have been very successful in helping students, often to obtain grades and offers well beyond the expectations of their schools.

Our philosophy is to teach every student a very simple structure, closely designed by reference to the mark scheme which will maximise the results achievable from their hard work. All of the tutors at Revision Hive are either current Uni students or recent graduates, and we understand that a relaxed and fun approach to tuition, combined with learning the vital strategies and techniques, is the perfect way to teach our students. Most importantly, we are all young, friendly, and relatable!

Revision Hive also offers a number of free resources for students, including revision sheets for GCSE and A Level exams, study resources, and more personal statement tips and tricks. We are building a student community on the website where people can ask questions and receive quick (and free) answers from fellow students or tutors.

If you are interested in checking out Revision Hive or simply want to get in touch with me, then visit the website:

www.revisionhive.com

Also, feel free to email me directly if you have any questions regarding this book or tuition opportunities:

Jonty.purvis@hotmail.co.uk

Foreword

Whilst at University, I worked as a tutor in my spare time, and noticed I was starting to get a lot of questions about the best way to draft a personal statement. I had enjoyed writing my own personal statement, but many people found it a stressful and difficult experience. After talking to admissions tutors, and looking critically at many statements, I realised that most students struggle to project their abilities and enthusiasm because they have no clear idea of how to put their ideas together in a coherent way. What is needed is a simple pattern in which the key 'selling points' for every student can easily be made. This led me to develop my '5 step formula' for personal statement writing (see Chapter 9 for a summary). Many of my students have already benefited from this formula, and it can really help you to structure your statement.

This book will explain the '5 step formula' for writing a personal statement. It is a quick and simple guide to help you get started in structuring your personal statement, and also provides a number of tips on how to impress the admissions tutors.

This book also contains many real personal statement examples, produced with the permission of the students who wrote them. These examples, dating from 5 years ago to just last year, helped their students receive offers from some of the top universities in the country, and they thus provide a useful guide to the type of content which is needed in order to produce a successful personal statement.

Again, if you wish to contact me about private tuition, mock interviews, personal statement help, or any other questions, then please visit my website:

www.revisionhive.com

CONTENTS

1. INTRODUCTION

The personal statement is considered by most students to be a very scary and daunting task. Many people spend months writing, it, weeks reviewing it, and some even spend days crying about it. For a significant number of students, it is the first time they have had to write an official application letter for anything, let alone for something as important as university applications.

However, the personal statement is not something to stress about. This book has been written using information gathered from university lecturers and admissions tutors, school teachers, and private tutors. Through our step-by-step blueprint, we hope to give you all the information you need to write your personal statement as quickly and easily as possible.

One thing that sets this book apart from other personal statement guides is that it gives real examples to back up the points being made. It could be confusing, for example, to simply say: "For your 1st sentence, relate your subject to a wider issue". However, this book will always offer examples of what exactly this means, and how real students have used this exact technique in their own personal statements.

But what is the 5 step formula?

<u>5 Step Formula:</u>

1. **Introduction** (Chapter 4)
2. **Interests** (Chapter 5)
3. **Work Experience / Subject Activities** (Chapter 6)
4. **Extra-curricular** (Chapter 7)
5. **Conclusion** (Chapter 8)

If you simply want a summary of the '5 step formula' for structuring your personal statement, including examples of good paragraphs, then you can turn to Chapter 9. However, it is best read the entire book in order to gain a fuller understanding of how exactly to write and structure each paragraph of your statement.

This book will be split into 3 parts. Firstly, it will give a brief overview of the personal statement and why it is important. Secondly, it will offer a detailed 'five step formula' for writing your statement. Finally, it will give examples of different REAL personal statements (which the students used to gain offers from places such as Cambridge, LSE, and UCL). Overall, this book aims to build your confidence in personal statement writing, and give you the tools and knowledge to write an excellent personal statement without the stress.

2. WHAT IS A PERSONAL STATEMENT?

The personal statement is part of your application to university. When you apply to university through the UCAS website (or other application platforms for countries outside the UK), you are required to submit a personal statement, maximum 4000 characters in length, along with other information such as your exam grades and contact information.

The UCAS website states that the personal statement is "a chance for you to articulate why you'd like to study a particular course or subject". This is very important to remember. The statement should not include your entire life story, your hopes and dreams, or every medal you have won since you were five years old (although some aspects of these can be used)! The personal statement should be much more specific. It is a brief summary of your subject choice, including: Why you chose the subject, what particularly interests you about the subject, how your skills will help you study the subject, and what other 'value' you can bring to the subject and to the university. The sooner you start thinking about the personal statement in terms of the SUBJECT you are studying, the better.

But why is a personal statement needed? Well, most universities use it as 'one part' of the admissions process. They combine your statement with your school references, your previous / predicted grades, and any other specific tests you are required to take. There is no consensus as to the importance of the personal statement in comparison to the other parts of the application. Some academic staff have suggested how the statement only plays a small role, and it is your grades which mostly decide if you will be made an offer. Others, however, claim that it is a crucial part of the application.

If you are a medic, Oxbridge applicant, or at any university or course which requires an interview, then the personal statement also has a secondary role. Whatever is said on the statement can guide the questions you could be asked at interview, and this makes it doubly important. If you have interesting parts to your statement which you can talk about, it could make your interview much stronger than if you have a bland statement which the interviewer does not want to ask about. This will be discussed in more detail in Chapter 10.

Overall, whilst the precise importance of the personal statement will vary, it certainly does affect whether or not your application will be successful. This means that it is certainly worth making sure your personal statement it is the best piece of writing you are capable of.

3. THE 1ST SENTENCE

The 1st sentence is by far the hardest part of the personal statement. It is also one of the most important parts. If you begin well, then the admissions tutor will be more positive about your application as they read the rest of your statement, and their overall impression of you could be improved as a result.

I have seen many people begin personal statements with a quote. Some admissions tutors like this, but many do not. Personally, I don't think it is worth the risk. More often than not, a quote (which is after all by definition someone else's words not your own) can sound contrived or even cheesy, when in reality the tutor wants your genuine personality to shine through.

There are 2 extremely effective ways in which you can start a personal statement:

One technique is to relate your subject to a wider issue. Is there an interesting debate within your topic you can bring up, or future trends which you could discuss in relation to the topic?

Examples:

1. *"With an ageing population and increasing constraints being placed on the NHS, the medical profession in the UK is entering a turbulent era".* *(Medicine)*

2. *"In the increasingly complex and globalised nature of the world today, a knowledge of marketing is crucial in being able to successfully navigate through the various challenges businesses may face". (Marketing)*

3. *"The world is confronted by huge problems caused by rapid and complex changes within societies and in the environment, particularly those resulting from globalisation and climate change" (Geography)*

These openers are very effective as they show exactly why you think your subject is important. All of them help lead into the next sentence, which will probably be discussing how you feel you can combat these challenges through your study of the subject. Moreover, relating your subject to wider issues shows that you have a deeper understanding of global and national processes and debates, something which university tutors are themselves interested in.

The other way to start a statement is to relate your subject to your own personal experiences straight away. This should be done anyway throughout your statement, so it is not necessary to begin with this, but it can be effective if done well. This method can involve either talking about what your subject means to you, or defining your subject in your own way.

Examples:

1. *"When I enlisted in the Singapore Armed Forces, I was appalled to discover that homosexual soldiers are deemed to be mentally disturbed." (Law)*

2. *"Relationships, perspectives and solutions – to me that is the study of geography" (Geography)*

3. *"Since I was a young child, my teachers were the one consistent element in my learning environment" (Education)*

Whilst these openers are all quite different, they all give a personal touch which relates to their subject, either through how they personally define their subject (number 2), or how their subject is important to them (numbers 1 and 3).

Whatever method you choose, try to make your opener interesting. Discussing controversial (not too controversial) and trending topics is very interesting as it suggests you have a complex understanding of the subject area. Similarly, discussing the subject from a personal perspective is also interesting as it offers a unique viewpoint that the tutor may not have heard before. Either way, once you have completed your first sentence, the rest of the personal statement becomes much easier.

4. THE INTRODUCTION PARAGRAPH

After your first sentence, you still have the rest of the introduction to finish. Whilst the exact content of your introduction depends on how you wrote your 1st sentence, all introductions should do the same thing: Introduce your interest in the subject. This should cover 3 key areas: (a) Why is your subject important, (b) what in particular interests you, and (c) why you want to study the subject further at university.

If your 1st sentence discussed a wider issue / problem your subject faces, then explain how you are interested in these issues and want to help solve them. If your 1st sentence discussed your personal experience with the subject, say how this has led you to want to study the subject in greater detail. Whatever the case, you need to show why you think your subject is important to study at university.

Most importantly, your introduction must introduce a particular topic / multiple topics within your subject that particularly interest you. This will help make your statement stand out, and can nicely lead on to your second paragraph where you will discuss these specific interests in more detail.

Here are some examples of good personal statement introductions:

1. *The world is confronted by huge problems caused by rapid and complex changes within societies and in the environment, particularly those resulting from globalisation and climate change. Addressing these issues not only requires more profound research into the underlying causes and what can be done about them, but a proper knowledge and understanding of those causes amongst the public. It is disturbing that on many important issues people, including politicians, seem to develop opinions based on myth and prejudice, rather than the available facts. The denial of global warming and the 'knee-jerk' opposition to fracking are good examples of this phenomenon. For this reason I believe strongly that a proper education, particularly in the field of geography, is vital to all those responsible for making decisions about our future.* **(Education with Geography)**

2. *With an ageing population and increasing constraints being placed on the NHS, the medical profession in the UK is entering a turbulent era. To combat this, medicine must discover new innovations and improve its efficiency in order to provide the best possible care for future generations. I am extremely interested by these challenging issues, and the analytical and problem-solving nature of Medicine as a subject.* **(Medicine)**

3. *I have always wondered how the purchase of goods in one part of the world could affect individuals in another part of the world. Rapid globalisation is causing the global financial system to become increasingly interdependent, and the way in which micro transactions can impact wider socioeconomic processes is extremely interesting to me. Such globalisation is leading to severe challenges, with inequality, austerity, and neoliberal policies causing significant issues across the world. I believe a strong understanding of economics is necessary in order to effectively understand these complex problems, and help find possible solutions (**Economics**).*

Each of these introductions introduces key areas of interest within the topic which can be discussed later in the statement:

1. Fake news, global warming, fracking (Geography)
2. NHS, medical efficiency, analytical / problem-solving aspects (Medicine)
3. Globalisation, inequality, neoliberalism (Economics)

It is crucial not to go into detail in the introduction. You are simply explaining why you think your subject is important, what in particular interests you, and why you want to study the subject further at university.

5. INTERESTS

The second and third paragraphs of your personal statement are interchangeable, and their order entirely depends on the subject you are doing. If you are studying Medicine, Law, Education, or another subject where work experience is vital, then your second paragraph should be about your work experience. However, for most statements and subjects, I would suggest that work experience should go in the third paragraph.

The second paragraph, therefore, should go into more detail about **your interests and what you have done to explore them**, including books you have read or talks you have attended. This should be the longest paragraph of your personal statement, and should tell a **story** about your interests (as explained later in this chapter).

The basic idea here is to take some of your interests discussed in the introduction and go into more detail about them, give some of your thoughts on the issues (but not controversial thoughts!), and outline **how** you have shown your interest.

This is where you have to get a little creative. You may not have read a book or article on an exact topic that you mentioned in your introduction, but you can always choose a book that is similar to your topic and relate it somehow. The best thing to do, however, is to google some of the key / most popular books within your subject area, order them from Amazon, and then write about them briefly in this paragraph. You can then start to build sentences such as this:

"Reading ... (insert book name here) ... helped me realise ... (insert your thoughts on the topic here) ... This inspired me to research the topic further, and I attended ... (insert name of talk / lecture / debate / another book here)".

The trick here, and the most important thing you should learn from this chapter, is to start to build a **story** which shows your deep interest in the subject. Stories are notoriously more interesting, appealing, and memorable than straight facts. So turn your facts into a story. Do not simply say: "I read this, I saw this, I attended this". That is extremely boring. You rather want to tell a story about how you first saw something as a young child, or you first heard about something on the news, or you first read an article in Year 11, and that **inspired** you to research the issue further: So you read more books about the subject, attended more lectures, and started to form interesting opinions on the topic.

Here are some examples of excellent second paragraphs for Geography personal statements. But which one do you think tells the best story?

1. *In my first year of school sixth form, I covered 'Populations', 'Globalisation', 'Water & Carbon Cycles' and 'Hot Desert Environments' – all relating to development. This led me to read Collier's 'Bottom Billion' which discusses the socioeconomic*

implications of countries' physical limitations, such as being landlocked. Having gained an insight into Africa's geopolitics I was keen to explore different areas, coming across Reeve's 'The Coffee Trail' – which looked at Vietnam's rising influence on the coffee trade. What interested me the most was the impact of Vietnam's success; fuelling disparities regarding basics, such as food, in other producing countries like Kenya. Moreover, speaking to a PhD student at Oxford about the 'unfair' trade of Fairtrade brands highlighted the complexities of developing a totally equal trade system. Interest in inequalities led to further research in contemporary issues, especially in the Global North as highlighted in Dorling's 'The Equality Effect' lecture. Hearing his theories on the United Kingdom (UK) being the most unequal society in Europe brought the ideas of inequality closer to home and made it more approachable.

2. *Over the course of my A Level studies, my interest in Human Geography has grown enormously. I particularly enjoyed looking in detail at the effect of Globalisation in the High Street as part of my Open University (YASS) module. I am also intrigued by the debate on population growth. Reading the conflicting arguments put forward by Stephen Emmott and Danny Dorling in their rival books about the potential population crisis of the next few*

decades has inspired me to want to study this issue further.

3. *Geography as a subject has always intrigued me, however it was only after I attended a variety of lectures at school that I realised the scale and importance of Geography in the real world. Dr Clare Herrick's talk on the geography of obesity, and Dr Jan Axmacher's discussion on biodiversity are two examples of this. They helped me realise that there can be a geography of almost anything, and that it is not just an academic subject, but a certain way of looking at the world.*

Whilst all 3 of these paragraphs offer an intriguing insight into the student's interest in the subject, it is the 1st of these paragraphs which tells the best **story.** Having been interested in certain topics from his A Level, such as geopolitics, this student went on a '**journey**' where they read 2 different books and even spoke to an Oxford student about their ideas. Not only does this student outline their journey, but they also gave some of their opinions on complex issues, showing a deep level of understanding and passion for the subject which many students fail to do in their personal statements. Overall, this paragraph has achieved the 4 key aspects that are required in a second paragraph:

1. Give more detail on specific interests relating to the subject.

2. Give personal thoughts and opinions on these issues

3. Give examples of how you have shown your interest e.g readings, talks, debates.

4. Tell a **story** which shows how your interest in the subject has developed over time, using phrases such as 'this led me to…'.

6. WORK EXPERIENCE / SUBJECT ACTIVITIES

The third paragraph should be more **activity** related. It should suggest how you have taken an active interest in your subject, rather than simply reading books. This paragraph should again tell a **story** about how these activities helped develop a strong interest in the subject. It should include at least one of these:

1. Work experience

2. Volunteering

3. Subject-specific event / course / competition you have attended or entered

This paragraph can basically go one of two ways. It can either be entirely focused around work experience / volunteering, or it can be an extension of the previous 'interests' paragraph, where you go more in depth about your interest in the subject and how you explored that interest through different activities.

For some students, particularly those who are studying a subject which lacks obvious work experience options (e.g Geography, History, English, etc.), then this third paragraph may be fairly similar to the second paragraph. These students should bring in more specific activities (such as events / competitions / extra courses) they have completed which relate to their course.

However most students, including those stated above, should try to include some form of work experience or volunteering in this paragraph. The important thing here is to relate your activities to the course, either directly (e.g you worked at a law firm and you are applying for law), or indirectly, by showing how the skills that you learnt can be transferred to help you in your course (e.g you volunteered at a homeless shelter and learnt how to stay calm under pressure, something which could be useful in a courtroom).

Volunteering is highly valued by many admissions tutors, as it shows a student is empathetic, well-rounded, and hard-working. If you have yet to complete any volunteering, I would suggest you volunteer somewhere which could be related to your subject for at least a few days, in order for you to gain valuable experience and be able to offer a more appealing and relatable personal statement.

Work experience is also a crucial thing to include. Obviously for medicine, law, or other degrees where work experience is vital, then much more time should be spent writing about your experience. But whatever subject you are doing, work experience shows you are hard–working and dedicated.

When writing about work experience or volunteering, try to give **specific examples** of times which were extremely **memorable, heart-warming, difficult, or eye-opening.** This not only helps to make the work experience more 'believable', but also shows your passion for the subject and exemplifies the skills you have learnt which could be used in your degree.

Example (Medicine):

My experiences working in a number of medical environments have helped mould my interest in the discipline. Shadowing several GPs at the Wendover Health Centre over two weeks was an incredibly eye-opening experience. It allowed me to see a variety of people from different backgrounds, and experience numerous aspects of GP work. One of the most interesting patients was a young firefighter who had previously worked in the armed forces. He battled with anxiety and depression due to his experiences in the army, and struggled opening up to people. Despite these difficulties the doctor was able to successfully engage with him and refer him to an appropriate mental health group; this helped me realise the importance of compassion and empathy in the medical field. It also sparked my interest in military cases, and I later spent a week working at Pirbright Army Training Centre. This was a challenging but engaging placement where I was able to observe a variety of different jobs, showing me just how extensive the medical profession can be.

This is an excellent work-experience paragraph for many reasons. Firstly, it gives specific examples of different scenarios which occurred, such as the 'young firefighter'. This scenario includes many different factors: A memorable experience (the firefighter), A heart-warming moment (helped his mental health), a difficult situation (struggled to open up about depression), and an eye-opening result ("helped me realise the importance of compassion and empathy in the medical field").

This paragraph also tells a good **story**, as this one experience "sparked [an] interest in military cases" and led to the student working at a medical army centre. This shows how interested the student is in the subject, and how they have taken ACTION to fulfil that interest (work at Pirbright Army Centre after the firefighter experience).

Finally, this paragraph relates the work experience to the subject they are applying for (Medicine). It makes multiple references to medicine as a discipline, such as "empathy in the medial field" and "how extensive the medical profession can be". This is fairly easy to do as the student is studying medicine and undertook work experience at a surgery, but it is not always so easy.

Let us think of a more difficult scenario: You are studying Geography but undertook work experience in a bank. This makes it even more important to try to relate the work experience to the subject you are applying for. For example, you could suggest how your work at the bank involved an interesting mix of quantitative data crunching and qualitative customer research reports. This reflects the dual nature of Physical and Human Geography respectively, and shows how you have developed skills in both data analysis and report / essay writing, which is a crucial combination for any Geography student.

In summary, this paragraph should include these key areas:

- Talk about at least one of: Work experience, volunteering, or subject-related activities such as competitions or events you attended.

- Mention a particular moment during your work experience / event which really inspired you to learn more. This moment should be at least one of: Memorable, heart-warming, difficult, or eye-opening.

- Tell a story again: E.g You experienced... during your work experience, you then became particularly interested in... and volunteered at... as a result.

7. EXTRA-CURRICULAR

This is the 'personal paragraph', which should be fairly short (no more than 100 words) and concentrate on the extra-curricular activities which make you unique and appealing to a university. This section can include: Duke of Edinburgh, Young Enterprise, sports, societies, hobbies, responsibilities (looking after a vulnerable person), I.T / tech abilities, notable life experiences, etc. Whatever you write about, there is one rule that should always be followed in this paragraph: Don't mention something unless it shows your skills or personality!

The two key goals of this paragraph:

1. Show your skills, talents, and abilities through your various extra-curricular activities.

2. Give more of a 'human-face' to your personal statement, helping your personality to shine through.

The two goals explained:

1. Your skills should always be made clear. Obviously, if you say you are part of the debate team and won a national debating competition, then this shows your skills. You do not have to say: "I am part of a national debate team and won a national debating

completion, *which shows my communication skills*". The last part is unnecessary, as you obviously have communication skills if you won a debating competition. However, if you want to say how you play football every week, then you will need to explain more clearly how this shows your skills. For example: "I play football every week for my local team, *and this has taught me crucial time-management skills, as well as improving my ability to work in a team*". Here, the last part is very necessary, as it shows the tutor how your weekly football can be relevant to your university course.

2. The 'human-face' is very important. You want to give the admissions tutor a good understanding of your character in this paragraph. You want them to believe that you are a well-rounded student, who is not only academically bright, but also skilful in other areas which could be beneficial to the university. You want to show them that you are not an 'academic robot', but are a fun and charismatic individual who will be a delight to teach. You want to show them your key skills which are transferrable and could help you during your degree.

What skills should be mentioned?

A good way to start this paragraph is to search for your course on the different university websites and note down the 'skills' that the university implies you should have. For example, if the website states that your course has lots of group-work, then maybe teamwork would be a useful thing to mention in this paragraph. If your course has presentations, then maybe confidence and communication will be good things to show in this paragraph. If you have a 'creativity' or 'innovation' module, then you should give examples of your creative skills in this paragraph.

Here is a list of some of the skills that you should try to show in this paragraph:

- Adaptability
- Communication
- Confidence
- Creativity
- Efficiency
- Empathy
- Hard-work
- Leadership
- Organisation
- Positivity
- Problem solving
- Responsibility
- Team-work
- Time-management
- Working under pressure

Obviously you cannot mention all of these skills in this

paragraph, but you should try to include at least 2-3 to show the university that you are a skilled and able student.

Here are some real examples of extra-curricular paragraphs in personal statements: Which do you think is the best?

1. *Outside of academics, I enjoy a range of different activities. Being a member of my school Fives team has certainly improved my teamwork skills, and completing my Gold DofE award was an incredible experience which showed me the value of determination in challenging situations. In fact, I now volunteer with mentoring Bronze DofE pupils, which has helped develop my confidence and leadership.* (Medicine)

2. *I actively engage with inequalities in my own life, evident in my leadership of the LGBT+ Network where I am currently spearheading the creation of a local network to help schools engage with issues of discrimination. Debating, Model UN, netball, martial arts and writing are all interests I currently pursue and are interests that I intend to continue pursuing during my time at university.* (Politics)

3. *Outside of academics, I enjoy playing a variety of sports. I founded and led the Homerton College Croquet team at university, which greatly*

improved my leadership and management skills. I have also played rugby for college and club for most of my life, which has taught me the importance of hard-work and teamwork when completing any group challenge. (Marketing)

4. *I am currently working full time as a 'Gap Student', helping with teaching and learning in the French and Geography departments in a primary school. I enjoy coaching the boys in sport using my rugby experience at school, club and county level and I also referee competitive matches. Outside work I volunteer as a Cub Scout leader. Working with children has been a hugely rewarding experience and I am considering the possibility of a career in teaching, educational policy or school administration.* (Education with Geography)

5. *In my spare time I volunteer in a local Maths class, helping struggling children with their work. This is a challenging yet rewarding experience, and has helped develop my organisational and concentration skills. I also enjoy playing the piano, which has helped teach me the importance of hard-work and practice to overcome challenges. I believe this will help me at university, where balancing work with other commitments is an important factor.* (Economics)

Important note: Some of these examples include work experience or volunteering which would usually be placed in the 3rd paragraph. However, if you are taking a highly academic subject, then as stated in the previous chapter it may be better to concentrate the 3rd third paragraph on your wider interests in the subject and the activities you have pursued to show your interest, rather than work experience. If this is the case, then your work experience can make a small appearance in the 4th paragraph. However, most students should try to include work experience and volunteering in the 3rd paragraph and leave the 4th paragraph for extra-curricular activities.

So which paragraph do you think is the best? Personally, I think numbers 1, 3, and 5 are the best. This might be considered strange as numbers 1, 3, and 5 probably have the least interesting content, however they present it in the best way. The paragraph with the strongest 'content' and the most potential is number 2, but this student has not effectively explained how their extra-curricular activities relate to their subject. The first sentence of number 2 is excellent, showing strong leadership skills and helping the students' personality and interests shine through. However, the next sentence is not very compelling:

"Debating, Model UN, netball, martial arts and writing are all interests I currently pursue and are interests that I intend to continue pursuing during my time at

university".

The student evidently has a broad range of interests and extra-curricular strengths which could be discussed. However, the student simply listed these activities and didn't explain how they are relevant in relation to their course.

This would have been a much better final section:

"I also enjoy debating, and recently took part in the Model UN conference in London. This was an incredibly challenging yet rewarding experience, and meeting hundreds of students from different cultures helped to significantly develop my communication and teamwork skills."

The student's 4th paragraph would then look like this:

"I actively engage with inequalities in my own life, evident in my leadership of the LGBT+ Network where I am currently spearheading the creation of a local network to help schools engage with issues of discrimination. I also enjoy debating, and recently took part in the Model UN conference in London. This was an incredibly challenging yet rewarding experience, and meeting hundreds of students from different cultures helped to significantly develop my communication and teamwork skills."

This would be an excellent 4th paragraph. It shows a number of different skills: Leadership, teamwork, communication, and confidence (implied). It also helps the student's personality shine through, giving a personal account of their struggles at the LGBT+ network and showing how they have taken an active interest in their passion for debating by attending the challenging Model UN conference. Overall, this paragraph covers both the student's skills and their personality, which are the two key aspects of a good 4th paragraph.

8. THE CONCLUSION

The 5th and final paragraph should conclude your personal statement. This should be the shortest paragraph of the statement, and should not simply 'summarise' what you have said throughout, as that is pointless and a waste of characters. Rather, the conclusion should return back to your interest in the course.

The conclusion should have 3 sections:

1. Reiterate why you are interested in studying the subject at university.
2. Briefly discuss your future aspirations and how this subject will help you achieve your future goals / job.
3. Say something interesting and memorable which reflects your personality / view of the world.

The conclusion should be no more than 3 sentences, which means you can only really spend 1 sentence on each section. It is important to remember than the conclusion is probably the least important part of the personal statement, so do not waste too much time worrying about it, but you should still try to make an impression on the admissions tutor with it.

The 1st section of the conclusion should simply reiterate your interest in the subject. This should then be followed by a 2nd section discussing your future aspirations, and a 3rd section which includes a memorable statement which reflects your personality.

For example:

Overall, Marketing is a fascinatingly broad subject which I am interested to pursue further at university. It would allow me to develop my analytical, management, and creative skills, all of which would be extremely useful when joining a marketing team at any company, as well as in setting up my own business in the future.

Here, the 1st sentence explains the overall interest in the subject. The 2nd sentence begins by further explaining why the student wants to study the subject, before relating it to their future aspirations. The 2nd sentence ends with a hint about how the student sees his future career development. It reflects the students personality as an innovative individual with a slightly different perspective on the course than other students.

However, this conclusion could be improved, particularly the final section. Instead of simply saying they want to start a business, the student could say something like:

"Overall, Marketing is a fascinatingly broad subject which I am interested to pursue further at university. It would allow me to develop my analytical, management, and creative skills, all of which would be useful for my desired career in event marketing, as well as providing

me with the skills to begin my own business in the student events industry in the future, something which I am highly interested in".

This is much more unique and memorable, as it shows the student has a particular interest, 'event marketing', and even that they want to establish a student event company in the future. It is unlikely many other students, if any, will have given this response, and thus makes their personal statement stand out from the crowd.

9. HOW TO STRUCTURE YOUR PERSONAL STATEMENT: A SUMMARY

If you have completed everything in the previous chapters, then congratulations, you have finished your personal statement! This chapter will give a brief summary of how to structure your personal statement, using the 5 paragraph model discussed in this book.

Remember, if you are studying Medicine, Law, or another subject where work experience is crucial, then your 'work experience' paragraph should be your 2nd paragraph and your 'interests' paragraph should be your 3rd paragraph, whereas for everyone else it is the other way around.

Structure:

1. **Introduction** (80 words)

- Start with a compelling 1st sentence that relates your subject to a wider issue or to your personal experience.
- Outline some of your particular interests within your subject.

- Explain why your subject is important to study at university.

  Example: *The world is confronted by huge problems caused by rapid and complex changes within societies and in the environment, particularly those resulting from globalisation and climate change. Addressing these issues not only requires more profound research into the underlying causes and what can be done about them, but a proper knowledge and understanding of those causes amongst the public. For this reason I believe strongly that further education, particularly in the field of Geography, is vital to all those responsible for making decisions about our future.*

2. **Interests** (200 words)

- Give more detail on your specific interests.
- Give personal thoughts and opinions on your interests / issues in your subject.
- Give examples of how you have shown your interest e.g wider readings, lectures, events etc.
- Tell a story: E.g You learnt about... at A Level, this inspired you to read..., you really enjoyed this author so watched a lecture on..., now you are fascinated to learn more about... at university.

Example: *My initial interest in Geography was sparked by the 'spectacular' physical aspects of the subject. On a World Challenge expedition to Iceland in Year 9, I was awestruck by the bubbling hot pools, the geysers and the vast lava fields: the most tangible evidence of the dramatic forces operating within the earth I have ever seen. I wondered how a modern society could grow and develop in such an extreme tectonic environment. Over the course of the past two years, however, my interest in Human Geography has grown enormously. I particularly enjoyed looking in detail at the effect of Globalisation in the High Street as part of the Open University module which I took alongside my A Levels. This module also exposed me to the issues surrounding population growth, and intrigued me to further research the overpopulation debate. Reading the conflicting arguments put forward by Stephen Emmott and Danny Dorling in their rival books about the potential population crisis of the next few decades has led me to believe that Geography is a subject which is all about perspectives, and the 'right answer' to global problems is never as simple as it may first seem.*

3. **Work Experience / Activities** (200 words)

- Talk about at least one of: Work experience, volunteering, or subject-related activities such as competitions or events you attended.

- Mention a particular moment during your work experience / event which really inspired you to learn more. This moment should be at least one of: Memorable, heart-warming, difficult, or eye-opening.
- Tell a story again: E.g You experienced... during your work experience, you then became particularly interested in... and volunteered at... as a result.

Example: *My work-experience as an assistant Geography teacher on my gap year allowed me to view the subject in a completely new light. When discussing poverty, many of the students recalled personal experiences where someone they know has struggled to afford basic necessities such as food or rent. In fact, they were surprised that the textbooks only discussed poverty as an issue which exists in Africa or South America, and makes little mention of issues closer to home. This encouraged me to take more of an interest in UK inequalities, and reading 'The Violence of Austerity' by Cooper and Whyte opened my eyes to the current problems of food-banks and austerity which exist in the country today. After this, I attended The Times Festival of Education, and implored Michael Gove to modernize the study of Geography to illustrate contemporary UK issues.*

4. **Extra-Curricular** (100 words)

- Show your skills, talents, and abilities through your various extra-curricular activities. Explain / imply what skill you developed through each activity.
- Develop a 'human-face' to your personal statement by giving some insight into your personality and some things that make you unique.
- Try to show some of the skills your subject requires (see university websites for what skills they are looking for). Examples of skills: Adaptability, Communication, Organisation, Responsibility, Time-management etc.

Example: *I have a great interest in rugby, having played at school, club, and country level for many years, and I regularly volunteer to coach younger boys at my local club at weekends. This has taught me the importance of both positivity and leadership, and how these traits can complement each other in many different walks of life. I also volunteer as a Cub Scout leader. Working with children has been a hugely rewarding experience, improving my communication and organizational skills, and I am now considering the possibility of a career in teaching in the future.*

5. **Conclusion** (70 words)

- Reiterate why you are interested in studying the subject at university.
- Briefly discuss your future aspirations and how this subject will help you achieve your future goals / job.
- Say something interesting and memorable which reflects your personality / view of the world and makes your personal statement more unique.

Example: *I would relish the chance for a deeper research into Geography at university level. Rapid action is needed in order to try and negate the impacts of issues such as climate change, overpopulation, and inequalities. A stronger understanding of geographical principles would give me the skills and knowledge I need to make a positive impact to society, and could help drive me towards a future career in teaching or public policy.*

10. FREQUENTLY ASKED QUESTIONS

• What is the word count of a personal statement?

The personal statement has a character count, rather than a word count, which is usually 4000 characters (including spaces). This usually means the personal statement should be 600-650 words. I suggest the following word count: Introduction (80), Interests (200), Work-Experience (200), Extra-curricular (100), Conclusion (70). However, it is completely up to you. If you have something really interesting to talk about for your work-experience paragraph, then maybe that should be longer. Once you have written your personal statement, paste it into the UCAS form (or whichever application form you are using), and you should be told if you are over the character count or not.

• How do I cut the word count in a personal statement?

The first thing to do is to go through the statement and cut out any superfluous words or phrases, as well as changing any extremely long words for shorter ones.

After this, you may have to cut out specific smaller sections which are not as relevant. In particular, you should look at cutting down the conclusion and the extra-curricular paragraph, as these are 2 of the least important. Always ask a friend or family member for help on this, as they will often have a better idea of what should be cut!

- What if you are applying for different subjects at different universities?

This can be difficult, for example you might be applying for Philosophy at Bath and Sociology at Bristol. The best thing to do is make your personal statement less subject specific. Find some common themes across both subjects (such as essay writing, critical-thinking, politics books etc.) and write about these aspects, rather than mentioning the subject by name.

- How can your personal statement help with your interview?

The personal statement for Oxbridge applicants, Medics, and any other subject which requires an interview is extremely important. This is because you could be asked in your interview about anything you write in your personal statement. This means you must have a good knowledge on any topic area or book that you mention in your statement. Moreover, you should try to mention quite interesting and specific things in your personal statement, because this will catch the interviewer's attention and they will be more likely to ask you about this. Simply mention some specific topic areas / debates within your subject, revise a great deal about them, and be ready to flourish in your interview when they ask about it. Of course, the interviewers could ask you nothing about your personal statement, but they often do, and you must be prepared for this.

- How to write a Masters personal statement?

A Masters or PHD personal statement should follow a similar pattern to the classic undergrad personal statement. The major difference is that, rather than discussing A Levels or school, you should spend a little more time discussing your undergraduate degree in your 2nd paragraph, and what particular skills / interests you developed which drove you to apply for a Masters. In reality, however, the personal statement structure should remain fairly similar.

11. REAL PERSONAL STATEMENT EXAMPLES

Extracts from these personal statements have been used throughout this book, but I will list some of these personal statements in full here. The examples listed below are real statements from people who received offers from top universities such as Cambridge, LSE, and UCL. You will see the '5 part formula' being used successfully in each of these statements.

1. Geography

This Geography student received offers from multiple top universities, including Cambridge. The statement is structured extremely effectively, with their 'definition' of Geography being given in the first sentence, and the theme of finding 'solutions' running throughout the statement. The 3rd paragraph concentrates on an interesting volunteering experience, and the only part which could be improved is the 4th paragraph, something which was discussed and re-written in Chapter 7 of this book.

Relationships, perspectives and solutions – to me that is the study of geography. However, with the rising problems of global inequality, it appears we are lacking either the means or motivation to find solutions to the most significant global problems. I wish to study Geography at university to gain a greater understanding of the different issues affecting the world, and the potential solutions which could help to solve them.

The scope of geography as a discipline allowed to me to develop an interest in development and inequality geographies. In my first year, I covered 'Populations', 'Globalisation', 'Water & Carbon Cycles' and 'Hot Desert Environments' – all relating to development. This led me to read Collier's 'Bottom Billion' which discusses the socioeconomic implications of countries' physical limitations, such as being landlocked. Having gained an insight into Africa's geopolitics I was keen to explore different areas, coming across Reeve's 'The Coffee Trail' – which looked at Vietnam's rising influence on the coffee trade. What interested me the most was the impact of Vietnam's success; fueling disparities regarding basics, such as food, in other producing countries like Kenya. Moreover, speaking to a PhD student at Oxford about the 'unfair' trade of Fairtrade brands highlighted the complexities of developing a totally equal trade system. Interest in inequalities has led to further research into contemporary issues, especially in the Global North, as highlighted in Dorling's 'The Equality Effect' lecture. Hearing his theories on the United Kingdom (UK) being the most unequal society in Europe brought the ideas of inequality closer to home and showed me how poverty, even in the UK, has a shockingly devastating impact.

I have also explored issues of poverty outside of the UK. In 2014, on a family holiday to my parent's village in Bangladesh I was surprised to see the poverty that I had only ever had second-hand experience of from textbooks. This led me to volunteer at the village homeless shelter, which made me realise that no issue can be viewed in isolation, but instead there are various perspectives that must be accounted for to truly analyse and understand a situation. Due to the nature of patriarchy in Bangladesh, most residents in the shelter were women. This was an extremely eye-opening experience, and helped develop my awareness of other issues regarding gender inequality, such as the issues surrounding Female Genital Mutilation (FGM). In fact, after leaving Bangladesh, I had the opportunity to attend a lecture by Hibo Wardare on her experiences of FGM in Somalia, and the inequalities that allowed it to take place. Evidently poverty exists throughout the world, and its consequences, such as FGM, require greater international discussion in order to be prevented.

I actively engage with inequalities in my own life evident in my leadership of the LGBT+ Network where I am currently spearheading the creation of a local network to help schools engage with issues of discrimination. Debating, Model UN, netball, martial arts and writing are all interests I currently pursue and are interests that I intend to continue pursuing during my time in university.

The holistic nature of geography has most definitely facilitated my personal development and my understanding of the world I live in. I am highly interested to learn more about these important geographical issues, particularly the problems of inequality, through my studies at university. Hopefully this will give me the tools needed to try and find solutions to some of the most difficult problems the world is facing, and would allow me to work at an NGO in the future so that I can try to provide solutions to some of these issues.

2. Medicine

This student received interviews from various medical schools with help from this personal statement. As should always be done with a medical statement, the work experience section is the longest, and comes right after the introduction. Also, the way in which 'stories' are told in this statement is extremely impressive.

With an ageing population and increasing constraints being placed on the NHS, the medical profession in the UK is entering a turbulent era. To combat this, medicine must discover new innovations and improve its efficiency in order to provide the best possible care for future generations. I am extremely interested by these challenging issues, and the analytical and problem-solving nature of Medicine as a subject.

My experiences working in a number of medical environments have helped mould my interest in the discipline. Shadowing several GPs at the Wendover Health Centre over two weeks was an incredibly eye-opening experience. It allowed me to see a variety of people from different backgrounds, and experience numerous aspects of GP work. One of the most interesting patients was a young firefighter who had previously worked in the armed forces. He battled with anxiety and depression due to his experiences in the army, and struggled opening up to people. Despite these difficulties the doctor was able to successfully engage with him and refer him to an appropriate mental health group; this helped me realise the importance of compassion and empathy in the medical field. It also sparked my interest in military cases, and I later spent a week working at Pirbright Army Training Centre. This was a challenging but engaging placement where I was able to observe a variety of different jobs, showing me just how extensive the medical profession can be. I have also spent time working with more vulnerable patients. The Weston Project is a local initiative which supports GPs in looking after elderly people and helps to prevent unnecessary admissions. I worked with a team on a number of home visits, helping to improve my communication and organisation skills. I also regularly volunteer in a severely learning disabled home, looking after three young people with a variety of disabilities including down syndrome and cerebral palsy. This has been a very rewarding experience, and has shown me the importance of versatility and patience when working in a difficult environment.

My motivations for studying medicine have been particularly enhanced by a number of talks and workshops I have attended. From a more practical standpoint, Dr. Niall McCann's 'The Last Eden' provided an intriguing account into the life of a doctor, and the InvestIN Young Doctor Programme helped me explore the incredibly complex nature of surgery. Furthermore, I recently attended 'Operating Theatre Live' which allowed me to experience the fascinating nature of dissection first-hand. I also find the more theoretical side of Medicine to be extremely interesting. Reading 'Nature via Nurture' by Matt Ridley helped improve my understanding of evolutionary anthropology, and how environmental factors can relate to genes. Moreover, the 'Science Live Biology Lectures' in London gave me an insight into a number of interesting medical topics, including the issues of antibiotic resistance. This inspired me to explore this issue in greater detail, with articles such as 'The antibiotic course has had its day' (BMJ, 2017) providing an engaging debate on the issues surrounding medical drugs.

Outside of academics, I enjoy a range of different activities. Being a member of my school Fives team has certainly improved my teamwork skills, and completing my Gold DofE award was an incredible experience which showed me the value of determination in challenging situations. In fact, I now volunteer with mentoring Bronze DofE pupils, which has helped develop my confidence and leadership.

Overall, Medicine is an extremely broad subject encompassing both practical and theoretical elements. It allows for a career that has a huge variety of transferrable skills, but most importantly it would enable me to help others and give back to society, something which has always inspired my love for medicine.

3. Politics

This student applied for HSPS (Human, Social, and Political Sciences) at Cambridge University. As a more academic-style personal statement, their 3rd paragraph talks about the activities they have done which relate to their subject (such as public speaking), rather than specific work-experience. This is a perfectly acceptable way to write a 3rd paragraph, and comes across very effectively in their statement.

When I enlisted in the Singapore Armed Forces, I was appalled to discover that homosexual soldiers are deemed to be mentally disturbed. Such systematic discrimination extends to people of different faith, gender or colour worldwide. Indignant about the outrageous bigotry against fellow mankind, I wish to study Humans, Social and Political Sciences (HSPS) to understand the struggle for human rights through multiple lenses.

In the realm of domestic politics, human rights is particularly relevant to the examination of liberal democracy. Concerned about horizontal inequality such as the discrimination against the LGBT community, I read Kenji Yoshino's "Speak Now: Marriage Equality on Trial" which justified gay rights on the grounds of immutability, the telos of marriage and parenthood. Homophobia, I believe, is a social construct enforced by society's dominant perspectives; religion plays a significant role in nurturing certain values and construction of these prejudices. Hence, this year, I volunteered in PinkDot, Singapore's LGBT pride event, to speak up for LGBT Singaporeans. On reflection, I was embroiled in the moral quandary between gay rights and religious freedom. I then sought to read Obama's "The Audacity of Hope". By juxtaposing Yoshino's secularism with Obama's liberal pragmatism, I learnt that both religion and sexual orientation are indispensable to one's being. In our pluralistic democracy, it is essential to engage controversial religious doctrines to reconcile fundamental human rights with religious values. The case for human rights is extensive, and the best way to reach a nuanced understanding of the issue is a multidisciplinary study afforded by HSPS.

My interest in exploring social inequities includes income inequality; I believe human rights invariably encompass the right to economic development. Having read R. Balakrishnan's "Rethinking Economic Policy for Social Justice", I learnt to view poverty through the lens of human rights. One cannot achieve their civil and political rights without access to economic opportunities. Living in Singapore, where decadence exists abreast distress, literally, I am inspired to champion social mobility. As the top student from an average secondary school, I was invited twice to motivate the graduating cohort of my alma mater to strive for their dreams. In retrospect,

Singapore may be highly unequal, but with good education policies, our axiom of social mobility remains tenable; countries with severe income inequalities and poor educational prospects incapacitate social mobility, thus human rights of their citizen. In this case, I believe developed nations have a moral obligation to help poorer countries because of their exploitations and/or the collectivity of the human race.

I am passionate writer, and in my spare time I enjoy writing a variety of non-fiction, with my most recent paper on language acquisition being published in Springer. I have also been a regular member of my school's debate team, something which has taught me the value of listening to others as well as public speaking. Moreover, having to organise various debating events has shown me the importance of time-management and organisation, traits which are valuable in all aspects of life.

As an aspiring polyglot speaking English, Chinese and French, I believe my linguistic capabilities will enable me to conduct cross-cultural research with novel perspectives. Through the study of HSPS at university, I wish to better comprehend the subtleties of contemporary socio-political issues, in order to do my part for a more humane world.

4. Economics

This is a more simple personal statement, but does a good job in effectively ticking all the boxes the admissions tutors want to see. It shows a strong interest in the subject, a wide-variety of reading and work experience, and overall helped the candidate to achieve a number of offers from some top London universities.

I have always wondered how the purchase of goods in one part of the world could affect individuals in another part of the world. Rapid globalisation is causing the global financial system to become increasingly interdependent, and the way in which micro transactions can impact wider socioeconomic processes is extremely interesting. Such globalisation is leading to severe challenges, with inequality, austerity, and neoliberal policies causing significant issues across the world. I believe a strong understanding of economics is necessary in order to effectively understand these complex problems, and help find possible solutions.

I have often been fascinated by the various arguments put forward by economists, and have read widely across the subject. One of my favourite books is 'The Undercover Economist' by Tim HarFord, which outlines a number of interesting macroeconomic principles and makes a compelling case for laissez-faire economics. From a microeconomic perspective, 'Freakanomics' by Levitt and Dubner is also an excellent overview, and inspired me to think of economics not solely as a global principle, but a consistent part of our everyday lives. Whilst many of these books have interested me, they are often rather sensationalist in nature, and I am eager to study economics through a more academic lens at university. I am also interested in the many new developments and discussions taking place within the economics discipline. Reading Neuwirth's 'Stealth of Nations' demonstrated to me the huge significance of the informal economy, and how most economic transactions take place informally and without record. I believe a greater understanding of this economy is crucial to ensuring future prosperity across the globe. Equally, I have enjoyed reading the various arguments on cryptocurrencies, such as Chiu and Koeppl's paper 'The Economics of Cryptocurrencies', and am intrigued as to how much of a role these unregulated digital currencies could have on the economic discipline in the coming years.

My work-experience at Barclays Bank in London really helped drive my interest in economics. I was fascinated by the plethora of market research which takes place before any investments are made, including the efforts made to predict future trends and minimise risk. This work also showed me the importance of the financial sector to people's lives, and seeing the happiness of a local entrepreneur when they received their first loan after many failed applications was an unforgettable *experience. This work magnified how a combination of both qualitative and quantitative data skills are required for any successful economist, and the well-rounded nature of the subject is certainly one of the major aspects that excites me about studying it further at university.*

In my spare time I volunteer in a local Maths class, helping struggling children with their work. This is a challenging yet rewarding experience, and has helped develop my organisational and concentration skills. I also enjoy playing the piano, which has helped teach me the importance of hard-work and practice to overcome challenges. I believe this will help me at university, where balancing work with other commitments is an important factor.

Overall, economics is a subject which I am extremely thrilled to pursue further. Whilst my wider reading has helped me develop a broad understanding of the discipline, I am motivated to discover more about specific theories and develop my understanding of a variety of areas. Economics is a subject for the future, and one which I am eager to study for many more years.

Printed in Great Britain
by Amazon

27787555R00037